ALL YOU NEED TO KNOW AB... AM... ...ER

How to be an Explorer

Written by Emma Lynch

Contents

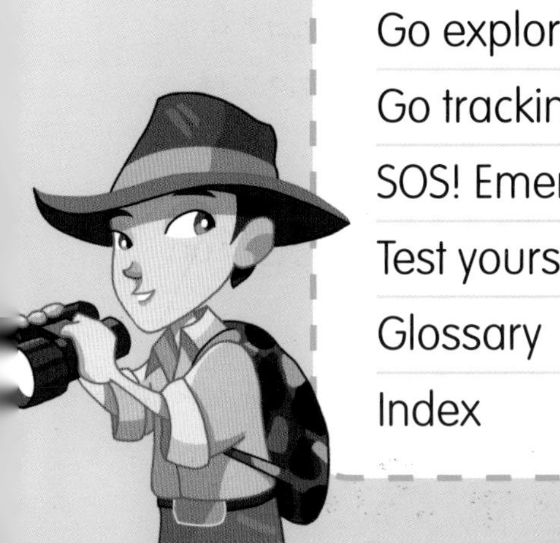

Have you got what it takes?

EXPLORERS WANTED

Brave and bold explorers are needed to discover new things about our world. There will be excitement and challenges. There may even be danger too.

You will get to:

- **travel the world and make incredible discoveries**
- **find places that no one has ever visited**
- **uncover lost worlds and people**
- **discover new plants, animals and sources of food.**

All this and more awaits you in the opportunity of a lifetime.

Explorer checklist

To become an explorer you will need to:

- ✔ learn how to cope in tough places and difficult situations
- ✔ be ready for extreme weather conditions
- ✔ pack the right things
- ✔ use maps to guide you to places
- ✔ know how to find food, water, shelter and heat
- ✔ record information about what you find
- ✔ cope with sudden change, unexpected situations and emergencies.

It takes time and training to be an explorer. After all, it's a dangerous job, so you need to know what you're doing. Read on and maybe one day you will make discoveries of your very own.

Why explore?

Starting out

Being an explorer is a truly adventurous job. So what makes some people take on the challenge?

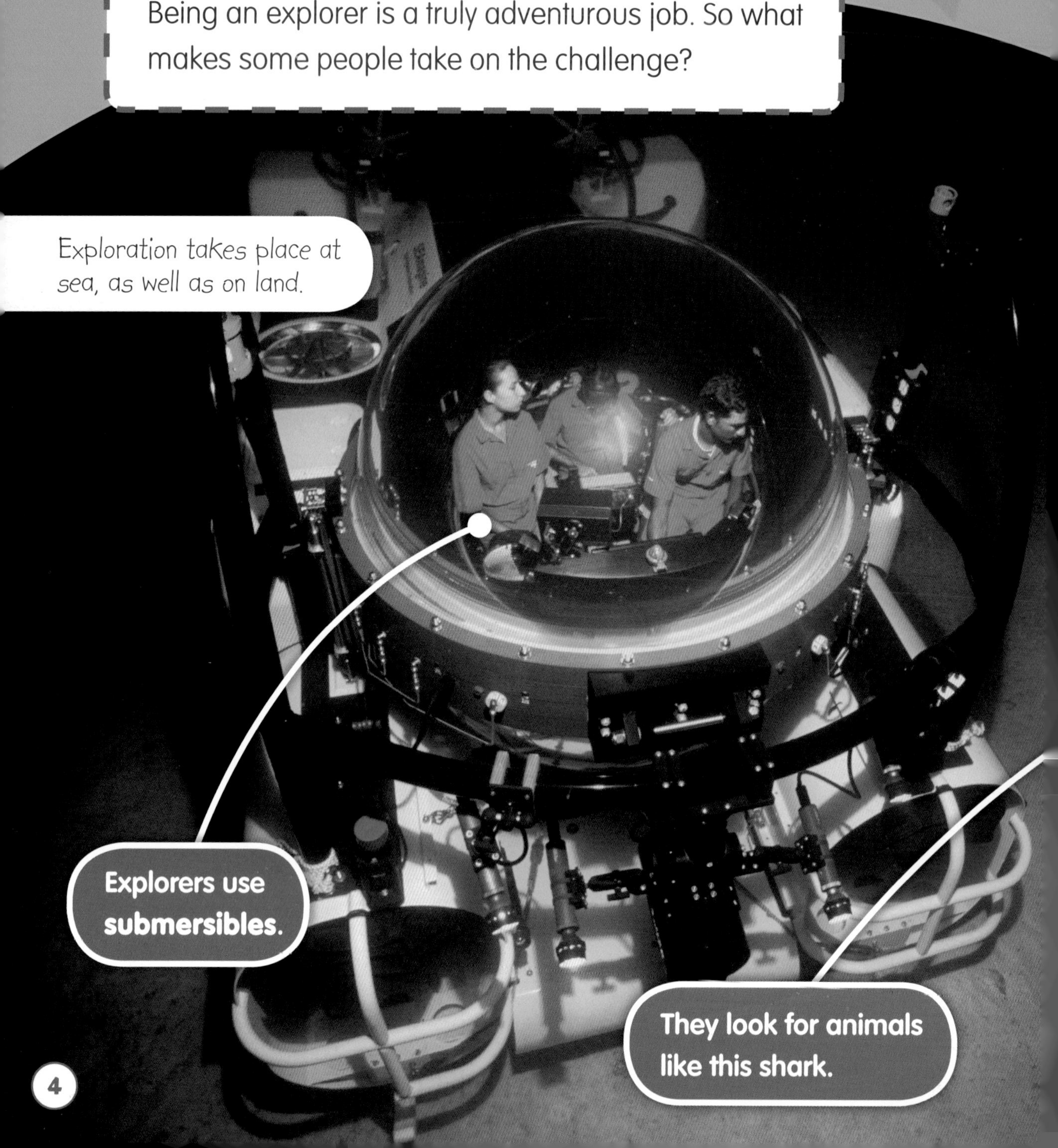

Exploration takes place at sea, as well as on land.

Explorers use submersibles.

They look for animals like this shark.

New challenges

Well, for many people it's the chance to discover new places, people, animals or plants. Others want to help protect places that are in danger, such as rainforests. Some want to see how they cope in tough conditions, such as the extreme cold of the Arctic.

Name: Sir Edmund Hillary
Born/Died: 20th July 1919 – 11th January 2008
Country: New Zealand

Mount Everest is the highest mountain in the world and many people have died trying to reach the top. On 29th May 1953, Sir Edmund Hillary and Tensing Norgay became the first climbers to reach the **summit**. Hillary said "It is not the mountain we conquer, but ourselves".

Sir Edmund carried extra oxygen to help him breathe near the summit.

No Way!

Some of the deepest parts of the sea have not yet been fully explored.

Where in the world?

The choice is yours

As an explorer you get to visit some of the world's most amazing places and toughest **habitats**.

Polar Regions

The Arctic is a huge area of ice around the North Pole. Antarctica is a large land mass found at the South Pole. Explorers go to study the animals in the Polar Regions and the effects of **global warming**.

Deserts

Deserts are the world's dry places, but they are not all covered with sand. Some are flat and stony and others are rocky and hilly. Explorers go to study how animals and plants manage to survive in such harsh and dry conditions.

Seas and oceans

Oceans cover 71% of the Earth. The biggest oceans are the Pacific, the Atlantic and the Indian Ocean. Explorers discover new life in the oceans every year.

Mountains

There are mountains all around the world. Some mountains stand alone and others are part of a 'range' or group of mountains. Explorers enjoy the challenge of conquering mountain summits.

Tropical rainforests

Tropical rainforests are found close to the **Equator**. The weather is warm and wet – perfect for plants. Explorers go to see the wide variety of animals and plants that live there.

Equator

When to go

Careful planning

There are a lot of things explorers need to consider to make sure they travel at the best times.

Animals travel too

Before they set off, explorers searching for animals need to know where to find them each season. Some animals **migrate**, moving to warmer places when the weather gets cold and then returning when it gets warmer.

Wildebeest can migrate 2800 km in search of grass and water, so you need to know the best time of year to see them.

The weather

Explorers often go to extreme habitats where the weather can make travel impossible.

Winter at the North and South Poles is not very welcoming.

Travel in Southeast Asia is harder in summer because of monsoon rain.

When should I visit the Amazon rainforest?

December to March	June to October
This is the rainiest time. The rivers will be higher so I will be able to travel by canoe.	These are the drier months. I won't be able to travel as far by canoe.
I will be able to see animals by the river's edge.	It will be easier to track animals because the land will be dry.

The Amazon is the largest rainforest in the world. It has the highest number of animal species too.

Pack your bags

Take the right things

Explorers pack different equipment and clothing for different places and different weather. However, there are some essential items that they must always pack for their safety and survival.

Your backpack should be comfortable to carry, and large enough for your kit. Test it out on a long walk before your trip.

Top Tip

Pack your backpack in reverse order, so that the things you need first will be at the top.

Essential items

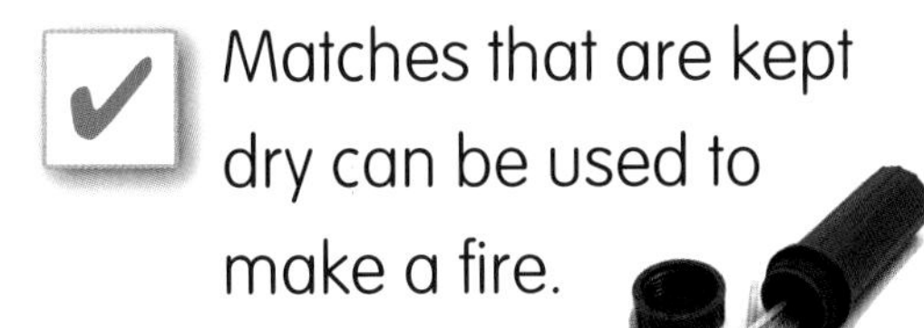

Matches that are kept dry can be used to make a fire.

A penknife can be used to cut wood and food.

A compass and map can help you find your way.

A torch shows people where you are and helps you see in the dark.

A whistle can be used to signal for help.

Always carry a water bottle.

String or cord is useful for making shelters.

A fleece will keep you warm and a waterproof coat will keep you dry.

Chocolate or high-energy snack bars are useful when you cannot find food.

Pack your first aid kit near the top so you can get to it quickly.

An explorer will also take:

- a camera
- a magnifying glass
- binoculars
- small bags to collect things
- a notebook and a pen.

Find your way

Which way?

Imagine you are deep in a forest. There are trees all around you. Which way do you go? When there are no signs or roads to follow, explorers use a compass and a map to **navigate**.

North, south, east or west?

A compass can help you work out where you are. The compass arrow always points to the direction of north. From here you can see the positions of east, south and west too. A good map will also show these positions.

On the map	Compass direction
Top	North (N)
Right	East (E)
Bottom	South (S)
Left	West (W)

Remember to keep your eyes open for clues when you are lost.

Some maps show the position of rivers, mountains, villages and railways.

Top Tip

A compass and a map can be lined up to guide you in the right direction.

How far is it?

Different maps are drawn to different scales. On one map 1 cm might show 1 km, and on another map 1 cm could show 10 km. To work out the distance between two places you need to know the scale of the map.

Many explorers use Global Positioning Systems (GPS) to help them navigate. A GPS uses information from satellites to show exactly where you are on Earth and how to get from where you are to where you want to be.

Try it!

Make a map for a friend to follow. Can you show north, south, east and west?

SOS! Lost

Be prepared

What would you do if you were lost and had no map or compass? Explorers would tell you to look for clues in the sky.

During the day

The Sun always rises in the east and sets in the west. At midday in the northern **hemisphere** the Sun points south. Explorers can use these markers like a compass.

Safety and the Sun

The Sun is an incredibly bright star. You must never look directly at it when using it to find your way.

At night

The North Star sits over the North Pole and it never changes its position. Explorers use the North Star to find north at night.

Top Tip

Sometimes if you are lost it is best to stay where you are and wait to be rescued.

No Way!

People have used the stars to navigate for thousands of years.

The Plough is shaped like a saucepan.

Try it!

To find the North Star, look for the stars that make the Plough. Imagine the line continuing upwards from the top star. This will lead you to the bright North Star.

Set up camp

Choose the right spot

When explorers have reached their destination or if it is getting dark, they need to set up camp. They have to be careful though – they don't want any nasty surprises!

The toilet area should be away from the tent, food and water.

The fire should be away from trees, so it does not start a forest fire.

Set up camp near water – you will need it for cleaning, cooking and drinking.

Put up the tent in a sheltered spot away from strong winds.

Level ground is best. Avoid places that are rocky, on a steep slope, or where an animal has been sheltering – it might come back!

Build the fire close to your tent. It should keep you warm but not be dangerous.

Bears have an amazing sense of smell. They can smell food from over 25 km away.

Food and rubbish attracts bears to campsites.

Set up camp quickly if bad weather is coming or night is falling.

Sometimes explorers have to camp in extreme places.

Top Tip

Be careful where you put your tent. You don't want to camp on an ant hill.

SOS! Take shelter

Do-it-yourself tent

Sometimes the worst happens and explorers have to survive without tents. They build emergency shelters out of any material they can find. Sometimes they even dig holes in the snow to shelter in.

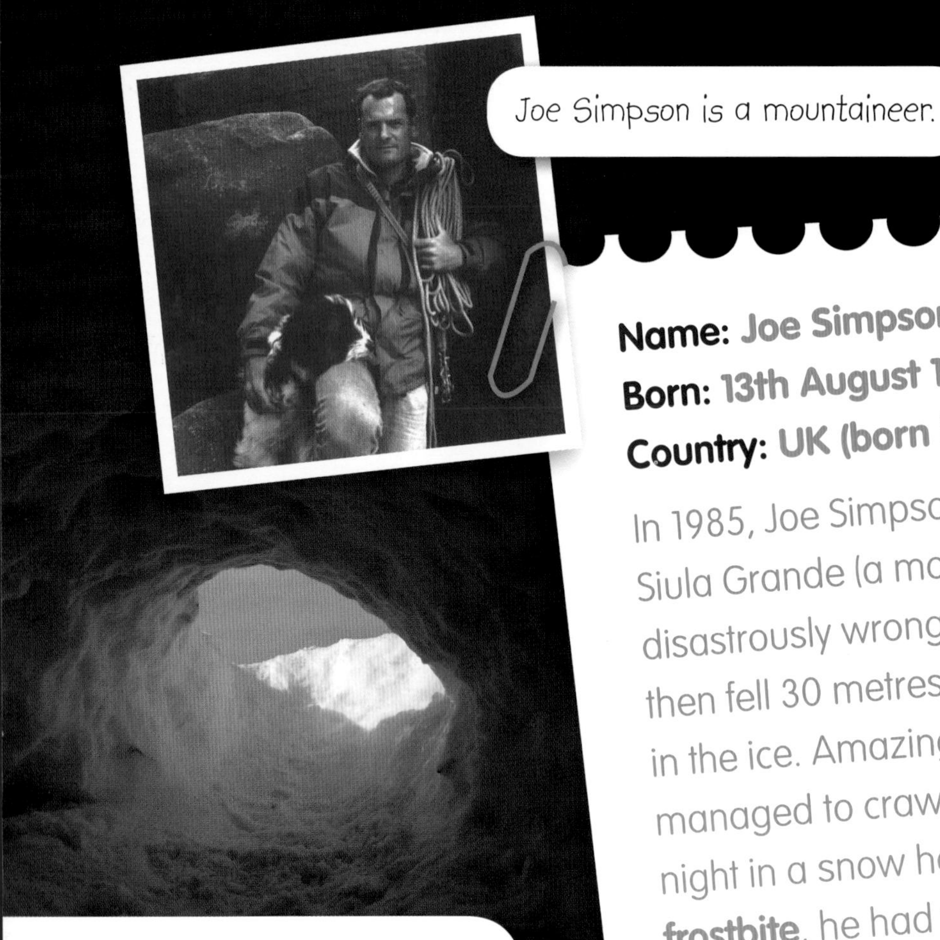

Joe Simpson is a mountaineer.

A snow hole provides shelter from the weather.

Name: Joe Simpson
Born: 13th August 1960
Country: UK (born in Malaysia)

In 1985, Joe Simpson's exploration of Siula Grande (a mountain in Peru) went disastrously wrong. Joe broke his leg, then fell 30 metres into a deep crack in the ice. Amazingly, he survived. Joe managed to crawl out and spent the night in a snow hole. Injured and with **frostbite**, he had to crawl and hop the six miles back to camp.

Build a shelter

Make sure your shelter faces away from the wind.

1 Find a strong branch to stand upright next to a tree.

2 Rest another branch between the top of the upright branch and the tree.

3 Lean long branches against the top branch and tie with string.

4 Add more branches as uprights at the sides and fasten with string.

5 Fill in the gaps with grass, bracken and large leaves.

Try it!

Try building your own emergency shelter next to a tree. Make sure your shelter is sturdy before you test it out!

Light a fire

Make a firebow

Fire is an essential part of survival. Explorers need fire to keep them warm, cook their food and keep away insects. Most explorers use matches to light fires, but there are other things they can use.

You can make a firebow using dry wood and string.

1 The handhold holds the drill in place.

2 The bow is pushed back and forwards. This spins the drill.

3 The drill spins against the fireboard.

4 The rubbing movement produces heat. A tiny **ember** is made.

5 The ember is added to dried grass and twigs to start a fire.

6 Blowing the ember gently, helps the fire burn.

Be fire safe

Take great care when building and lighting fires. Remember:

- Do not light fires near trees and plants – they might catch fire.
- Do not light a fire in very dry weather – it might spread and start a forest fire or grass fire.
- Children can help to build the fire, but only grown-ups should light fires.

No Way!

Explorers can use magnifying glasses to start fires too.

Without a fire, explorers would have to eat cold meals all the time.

SOS! Find food and drink

Which food is safe?

Sometimes explorers run out of food and need to know how to survive in a wilderness. They need to know which wild foods are safe to eat, otherwise they could become very ill. They might even die.

Top Tip
Explorers are very experienced. It is not safe for anyone else to find food this way.

Wild food

OK
- fruit
- nettles
- **SOME** berries and leaves (not all are safe)

Beware
- mushrooms – many are poisonous
- plants with thorns and spikes
- plants with shiny leaves – some are poisonous

Explorers only eat food they know is safe, such as blackberries.

How to trap water

If explorers are a long way from any streams, they have to find other ways of collecting water. One easy way is to trap the water plants produce.

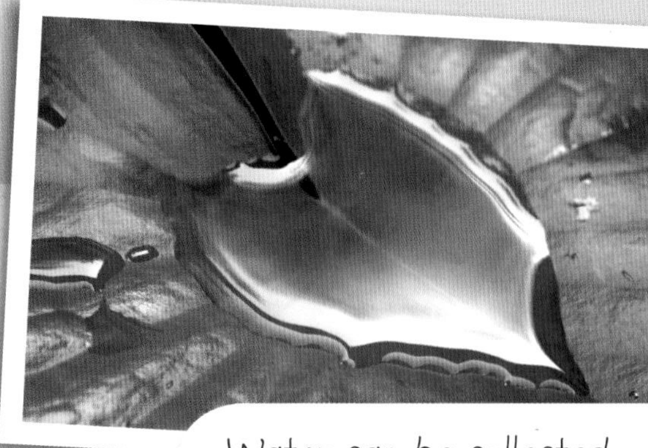

Water can be collected from leaves.

1 Tie a plastic bag over some leaves.

2 Wait for the sun to shine on the leaves.

3 Water in the plant will **evaporate** from the leaves.

4 Wait for the water to form **condensation** inside the bag.

5 Collect the water and drink it.

No Way!

People can survive without food for about three weeks, but they can only survive for three days without water.

Go exploring

Record it

Getting there is only part of the challenge. Explorers also collect information about plants, animals, people, places and weather. Sometimes they collect information using cameras, computers and sound-recording equipment. Sometimes, however, explorers just need to sit still and record what they see by sketching and writing.

An explorer studying an emperor penguin in Antarctica.

No Way!

Explorers in Australia discovered this new species of jellyfish 1400 metres below sea level.

When you see something unusual, keep a note of the place, date and time.

Place: Kinabalu National Park, Borneo

Date: 24th April 2011

Time: 11:03 a.m.

Record: Unusual plant found growing in moist soil at the bottom of Mount Kinabalu. Its stem is approximately 300 cm long and runs along the ground. Its leaves are large and green. Purplish pot-like traps grow from the stem and the plant traps insects that fall into them in order to eat them. The traps are approximately 20 cm tall and 12 cm wide.

purplish pot-like trap

Try it!

You don't have to travel far to be an explorer. You can explore a local park, your garden or your school grounds. Keep an explorer's diary and record where you go and what you see.

Go tracking

Seek the signs

Most animals are afraid of people and keep away from them. Explorers track animals by looking carefully for signs. They look for:

- animal tracks
- crushed plants or dropped food
- hair and feathers caught on branches
- scat (animal poo).

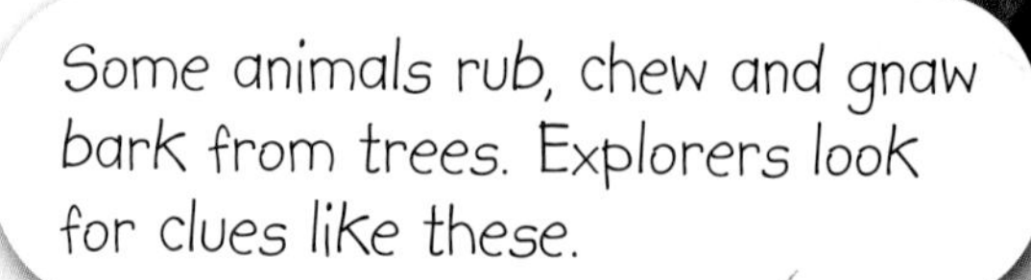

Some animals rub, chew and gnaw bark from trees. Explorers look for clues like these.

Animals often have regular travel routes and leave clues, such as footprints, along the way.

Deer leave clues such as their antlers, which they shed every year.

Hamish does research in the Polar Regions.

Name: Hamish Pritchard
Born: 1st December 1974
Country: UK

When Hamish was working in the Arctic he came across a polar bear. He stopped and watched the bear watch him. Eventually it wandered off. Later, however, the bear sneaked up on him! Hamish started up his **skidoo** and the noise scared the bear away. He didn't see the bear again, but Hamish knew it was still nearby when he saw a trail of giant footprints that had followed his.

Top Tip

If you meet animals in the wild keep your distance. Don't feed them or frighten them.

Polar bears usually eat seals, but anything they come across can be prey.

SOS! Emergency

First aid

When you are in an extreme habitat, anything can happen. Explorers need a good knowledge of first aid before they set off.

Problem	First aid
Insect bite or sting	Take out the sting. Cover with painkilling cream to soothe the itch.
Cuts	Clean the cut with an antiseptic wipe. Put a plaster on it.
Bruises	Place a cold, wet cloth on the bruise. Lift the limb with the bruise above the heart for 15 minutes. This reduces the size of the bruise.
Heat stroke (feeling dizzy, sick and weak with headache)	Move out of sunlight into a cool place. Undress and apply cool cloths. Lie down with feet higher than head. Drink lots of water.

These are some of the most common medical problems an explorer will face.

No Way!

Midges and mosquitoes hate Vitamin B1. Eat food like nuts and rice to keep the bugs away!

Only female mosquitoes bite.

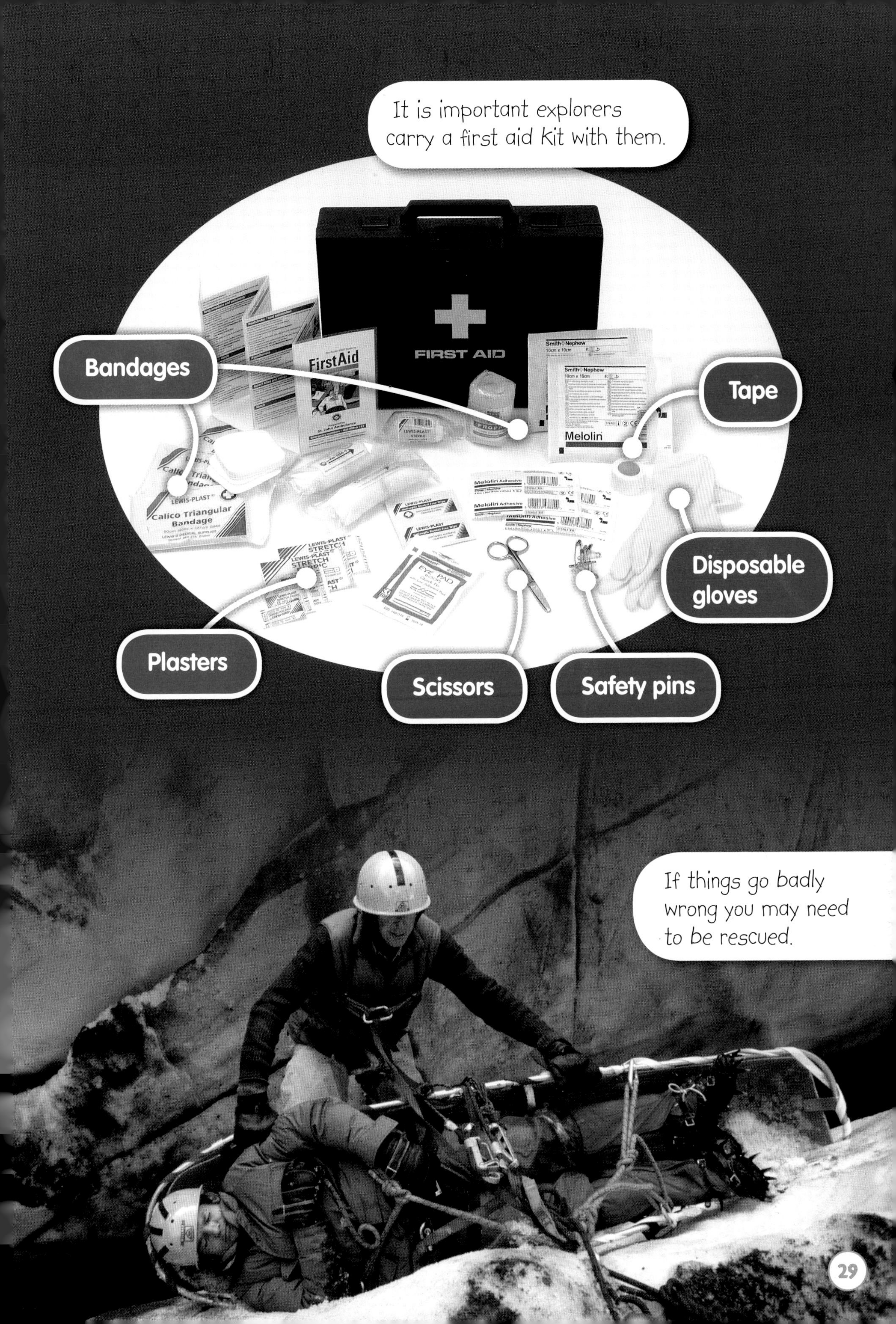
It is important explorers carry a first aid kit with them.
Bandages
Tape
Disposable gloves
Plasters
Scissors
Safety pins
FIRST AID
FirstAid
Melolin
Calico Triangular Bandage
LEWIS-PLAST
If things go badly wrong you may need to be rescued.

Test yourself

Do you think you have what it takes to be an explorer? Do this quiz to find out!

1

You are planning a trip. Do you:

A pack carefully, putting the things you will need first at the top of your backpack?

B pack the important things, but not in any order?

C pack lots of things into the largest rucksack you can find?

2

You are lost. Do you:

A save your energy and wait to be rescued?

B try to find your way by the Sun and stars?

C keep going, hoping you will find the place soon?

3

You are exploring but it is getting dark. Do you:

A look for a flat spot to put up your tent?

B put the tent up where you are?

C continue exploring – there is more you want to see?

4

You see an animal. Do you:

A keep still and quietly watch it?

B move quietly towards it?

C move towards it and try to pick it up?

5

You are exploring when you start to feel dizzy and sick. Do you:

A move into a cool place and drink lots of water?

B drink more water but keep going?

C keep going as there is no time to stop?

How did you do?

Mostly As
Congratulations, you are a born explorer!

Mostly Bs
Well done. You are on the right track, but there is more you could learn.

Mostly Cs
You have a lot to learn before you go out in the wilderness.

Glossary

condensation water that collects from the air on a cool surface

ember glowing, hot piece of wood or coal

Equator imaginary line around the middle of the Earth dividing it into North and South

evaporate when liquid turns to vapour

frostbite injury caused by extreme cold

global warming harmful rise in the world's temperature

habitat place where certain animals or plants live

hemisphere one half of the planet as divided by the Equator

migrate move from one place to another and settle there

navigate find your way

skidoo sledge with an engine

submersible vehicle that can explore underwater, like a submarine

summit highest point

Index